Selected Poems

BILL MANHIRE was born in New Zealand's southernmost city, Invercargill, in 1946. He was his country's inaugural Poet Laureate and has won the New Zealand Book Award for Poetry four times. He is a Professor Emeritus at Victoria University of Wellington, where he founded the celebrated creative writing programme and the International Institute of Modern Letters. His volume of short fiction, *South Pacific*, was published by Carcanet in 1994.

D1628197

700041034418

Portrait · Bill Manhire   Hotere '71

BILL MANHIRE

Selected Poems

CARCANET

First published in Great Britain in 2014 by
Carcanet Press Limited
Alliance House
Cross Street
Manchester M2 7AQ

www.carcanet.co.uk

First published in New Zealand in 2012 by
Victoria University Press
Victoria University of Wellington
PO Box 600 Wellington
New Zealand

Copyright © Bill Manhire 2012, 2014

The right of Bill Manhire to be identified as the author of this work has
been asserted by him in accordance with the Copyright, Designs and
Patents Act of 1988
All rights reserved

A CIP catalogue record for this book is available from the British Library

ISBN 978 1 84777 247 3

The publisher acknowledges financial assistance from Arts Council England

 Supported by
ARTS COUNCIL
ENGLAND

The cover and frontispiece portraits of Bill Manhire are by Ralph Hotere,
1971 and 1972 respectively. They were originally reproduced in Bill's first
book, *The Elaboration*, and in the privately printed *The Old Man's Example*,
and are used with permission.

Printed and bound in England by SRP Ltd, Exeter

Contents

from Zoetropes

from Milky Way Bar

from My Sunshine

from What to Call your Child

from Lifted

from The Victims of Lightning

New Poems

*I will place this paper in your hand
against the times you are alone:*

*my white one, my whitest one,
my pale, white stone.*

Love Poem

There is no question
of choice, but it takes
a long time.

Love's vacancies, the eye
& cavity, track
back to embraces

where the spine bends
& quietens
like smoke in the earth.

Your tongue, touching on song,
darkens all songs. Your touch
is almost a signature.

Poem

When we touch,
forests enter our bodies.

The dark wind shakes the branch.
The dark branch shakes the wind.

The Elaboration

There was a way out of here:
it went off in the night
licking its lips.

The door flaps like a great wing:
I make fists at the air
and long to weaken.

Ah, to visit you
is the plain thing,
and I shall not come to it.

The Spell

Each time I sneeze
the devil steps by me.
He pours the hours
into my wrists, minute
by minute.

That dream; in which I inhabit
my father's shoulder, a stale
whisky smell.

My friends send over their
daughters for safe-keeping. Such
commonplace girls,
all in aprons.

They smile
nevertheless, they manage it.
One is a bird, one a broken stone.

The Prayer

1
What do you take
away with you?

Here is the rain,
a second-hand miracle,
collapsing out of Heaven.

It is the language of
earth, lacking an audience,
but blessing the air.

What light it brings
with it, how far
it is.

*

I stayed a minute
& the garden
was full of voices.

2
I am tired again
while you are crossing

the river, on a bridge
six inches under water.

Small trees grow out of
the planks & shade the water.

Likewise, you are full of
good intentions
& shade the trees with your body.

3
Lord, Lord
in my favourite religion
You would have to be
a succession of dreams.

In each of them
I'd fall asleep,

scarred like a
rainbow, no doubt,
kissing the visible bone.

The Voyage

1
All night water laps
the hedges. I hold you in the middle
of the air.

2
Don't sleep
all night. It is pitch

black, but since
there is a vista, let

your throat be
the lantern.

3
Since there is
a window, let us

open it.

4
Let us dress
for a voyage. Let me

go out, with
your voice, to call for you.

Pavilion

The house was in the mountains,
perched on the moon's wrist.
We sung, we sang.
I have forgot it.

All day you drew ladies dancing on clouds,
one falling into the open mouth of a book.
It was in the mountains
and I prayed for the swan.
I forget it.

The red pavilion, the red pavilion.
A tree climbed back in its leaves.
Love, good morning,
your body was all freckles.

The Incision

Snow in the brain, under the skin.
Under the covers, bark and a few branches.
Locomotive nature is coming to find us,
waving its amenable flags. Not that
we are not also going out to find
it, but it is hardly necessary:

we always hated to be successful.
This must be a new episode in our lives,
side by side, with a certainty of capture,
while the leaves sink
into our shoulders like language,
words we are rumoured to live in.

And I don't know you, yawn in the heart,
even when you respect my wishes,
turning back into the steps
of nothing I ever wanted:
there, the lake choked with feathers,
there, the deep wings folded over.

The Poetry Reading

The green fields. The green fields.
How beautiful they are.
How beautiful they are.

This next poem is about the green fields
Which are to be found in England.
They contain certain small animals
Which have chosen to make their life there.

The public has constant access to them.
Not to the animals, as you might
Understandably think, but to the green fields
In which they have chosen to make their homes.

Ornaments

Water: you surface by multiplying.
Then the telephone calls start:
one very beautiful backstage actress,
two comparatively straightforward deliveries,
three blind mice.
Condemned or precocious, do you
really look that bad?

And because we are always
at the beach, going into the water,
I come home and stare at your ornaments:
it's dark and disgraceful
but it makes good sense, especially since
we had the new telephone installed,
the one I hear you hang up on.

I am hung up on you
if you will pardon the expression.
You submerge me like belief, like
tidal waves, and even the home is under.
'I hardly ever see you these days.
We never talk.' My excuse,
your excuse; late afternoon, the plans.

Last Sonnet

There is this photograph of you dancing
which keeps on arriving in the post.
Every morning I send out the dogs,
but they come back whimpering, broken-
boned: i.e.

the mails always get through.
Anne is laughing.
She turned into a tree.
Jane went to Europe,
a death to rocks and flowers.
Carol has had all her hair cut off.

What do you want, waving and
waving, your hands flung
right out of the picture?

Summer

1
It is so white.

It divides under the snow.
It wakes alone, a sensational pleasure.

2
Supposing this page is a paddock
under snow, or rather supposing
this page is snow

blanketing the paddock
then these lines

must be tracks in the whiteness
left by animals late at night.

Or fences, or trees
just risking the surface.

3
Possibly the bodies of lovers are also present,
though almost invisible to the naked eye.

4
See?

And occasionally, one supposes,
some marriage may be celebrated.

5
Or, this word may be a boulder,
or this, or this

or this, which is a stone,
on which the poet sits, somewhat alone,
saying, 'Hell, another masterpiece.'

It Is Nearly Summer

A rubber duck is paddling up the sky.
The world is a constant amazement,
always on the move.
It is nearly summer. It is nearly autumn.

On Originality

Poets, I want to follow them all,
out of the forest into the city
or out of the city into the forest.

The first one I throttle.
I remove his dagger
and tape it to my ankle in a shop doorway.
Then I step into the street
picking my nails.

I have a drink with a man
who loves young women.
Each line is a fresh corpse.

There is a girl with whom we make friends.
As he bends over her body
to remove the clothing
I slip the blade between his ribs.

Humming a melody, I take his gun.
I knot his scarf carelessly at my neck, and

I trail the next one into the country.
On the bank of a river I drill
a clean hole in his forehead.

Moved by poetry
I put his wallet in a plain envelope
and mail it to the widow.

I pocket his gun.
This is progress.
For instance, it is nearly dawn.

Now I slide a gun into the gun
and go out looking.

It is a difficult world.
Each word is another bruise.

This is my nest of weapons.
This is my lyrical foliage.

The Proposition

the week it
snowed, the day the
footpaths didn't matter,
I wanted to get

a number of things
straight, but didn't:
and the next day, when
people were out

again, driving, you said
let's take ourselves
off, into the country,
to a cave, or that

kind of expedition: I bent,
tentative, over the
table, and cracked my
knuckles: would you

care to be more
precise about whatever
it is you are
saying, I said

The Cinema

The Americans make many spectacular movies:
the surroundings of the town are beautiful,
the lake is enclosed by trees.

The other night we went
to a realistic, pitiless film. The spectators
cried, 'Encore!' Afterwards, we felt
we had risked everything.

Early in the morning, we weighed anchor.
We were on board a Russian steamer,
trying to find our sea-legs.

On shore there were many hardened criminals.
Many fields were under water,
many faces lit by summer lightning.

The Song

My body as an act of derision,
eating up the answers to life.
There is the bird-song, now,
elbowing through berries while
the hairs in my nose catch
at the little bits of existence.

And I know you go on living
because you need to be cared for.
I embrace you, I kiss you,
trusting in an ordered development,
watching the small explosions
under your wrists.

Oh we survive merely by good fortune,
by random appetite: going
outside to lie on our stomachs
as if we meant to swim in the earth,
floating near the dazed horizon,
giving this music into the light.

How to Take Off Your Clothes at the Picnic

It is hardly sensuous, but having
eaten all the cold meat and tomatoes
you forget to remove your trousers

and instead skip stones across the river
with some other man's wife
until, finally, the movement

of a small wind, no larger
than the reach of a finger
& thumb, makes it

impossible, carefully lifting off
every item of clothing.
Then you may share an apple and watch

from your side of the river
shoes & socks coming down
to rest on the other.

Some Epithets

1
Weary, stale, flat, unprofitable

world:
        hesitation conquers you,
your heart flies up.

What will these words be, without you?

2
What will you be,
what will you be

without those who care, assuming them?
Light, dark, quiet, loud,

soft rotten perfection.

3
Knowledge of them:

those who precede
and those who come after,

those who have knowledge of small flowers
and fall asleep in water

touching the soggy fists:
soaked and glorious, almost prevailing.

4
World, I mean,

world, world, world:
                    I mean
the stars:
            horizons, charts,

the gravel path:
                your birthdays
on the vigilant water.

The Trees

Barques we ride on over the sea:
we like to come in on the tide
alone and when it's morning, first
light shattering the bodies.
We want to go under completely,
a well-heeled relic of devotion.

Shapes in the dusk, the faithful
breathing, happens under leaves;
though what does it matter, let's suppose –
'under the circumstances' is where *we* are.
The truth is a requisite urge,
nobody's lover. Sweet sweetheart,

I have a good intention to be better.
I mean to be a silence,
a hair on the floor of the forest.
Why, I sometimes hope to be your pleasure,
the raft you swim out to in lake-water,
shaking a little when your body touches.

Contemplation of the Heavens
after Camille Flammarion

Innumerable worlds! We dream of them
Like the young girl dreaming
Who separates with regret from her cradle.
What cannot this adorable star
Announce to the tender & loving heart?

Is it the shy messenger
Of the happiness so long desired?
What secrets has it not surprised!
And who bears malice against it?

And yet, what is the earth?
Is not the great book of the heavens
Open for all to see?
Seek, talk, find out in your conversation.

A Song About the Moon

The moon lives by damaging the ocean
The moon lives in its nest of feathers
The moon lives in its nest of clamps
The moon lives by aching for marriage
The moon is dead, it has nothing to live for

The bodies are dangerous, you should not touch them
The bodies resemble our own, they belong together
The bodies are weapons, someone will die of them
The bodies will not lack for wings, someone will find them
The bodies are maimed but you will not remember

Do you still suffer terribly?
Do you always speak French?
Do you stare at the moon for you cannot forget it?
Do you long to be emptied of nothing but feathers?
Do you want to go on like this almost forever?

You must abandon everything after all
You must abandon nothing at least not yet
You must abandon hilarity
You must abandon your flags
You must abandon your pain, it is someone else's

You must abandon poetry for you cannot forget it
You must abandon poetry, it never existed
You must abandon poetry, it has always been fatal
It is like the moon, it is like your body
It is like the ocean, it is like your face

What It Means to be Naked

As you will know
the hands join hands to sing

and then you are naked.
Under the snow, the hands and chest

are draped, and with them the belly;
the thighs are pure bone

sunk without trace. Likewise
the eyes,

the mouth, the nose
sink in the face, while the teeth

are left surprised
by the pain which has vanished.

Also, as you will know,
the tongue leaves

its voice and taste to the snow
and the room at once

grows chilly. The hair,
of course, stays on the pillow.

Then the penis is removed
and shaved, as you will know,

and is buried subsequently
in snow: and this latter,

covering the earth as always,
as you will know,

and being no more
than the usual snow

under the snow
the snow will eat it.

Wingatui

Sit in the car with the headlights off.
Look out there now
where the yellow moon floats silks across the birdcage.
You might have touched that sky you lost.
You might have split that azure violin in two.

The Selenologist

Is gazing at the moon again.
He stares as usual through his optic lens,
The length of tube with glass at either end.
There, as it happens, is the outside cat;
And there are the fox & the flower & the star.
Among all these his life takes place.

There also is the river of light
Which moves past stars with golden rays
Too bright to contemplate or gaze upon.
The river itself begins in snow,
Far out in space. It travels under cloud,
And those who travel in the boat upon the river

Are pleased to hold beneath the cloud
Because there they are always safe.
(Of course, they will never again traverse
The space they have just left
And which they have just deserted forever,
They will never again embrace brothers or sisters:

They are looking for life on another planet.)
Imagine, before the selenologist was born
They were on their way. They dipped their oars
In cloud and thought of water. Even now
They hardly know if they are touching water
Through the cloud – for they are going with

The current anyway. They are unknown life
But not to each other. They know each other
By their voices and the songs they sing; yet
They can only assume the content of these songs,
The golden stars past which they journey,
They can only assume the water.

This is not strictly true
For they can almost guess at death.
They can imagine the faces, growing older;
Also, they know that if one should fall
From the boat, then it is one voice less;
And yet that such a splashing will confirm the water.

It is then they sing with purest pleasure.
The selenologist can hear across all space
The sound that water makes when violently displaced
And fancies he can hear them singing.
He knows that before he was conceived
This noise was on its way; and smiles

And sighs and gives the cat its supper.
He tells the story of the fox & the flower
& the star, he writes how happy all these are.
He sighs and writes: 'Life is motionless
In consequence of all the time it takes.'
He sighs and writes: 'Distance sets limits

Where our vision fails in space.'
He tries to imagine the boat upon the water
But can see only grass in a small field
By the river at the edge of cloud.
It is immense vegetation, fixed in place:
Green as emerald, soft like a lake.

Wulf

1
They take it from me:
            in the manner
of a gift

if danger moves in the earth
is the life given
is it love between us

2
Wulf: on that island
            — I on this other

shut into fens, a bone
in the neck of a savage

if danger moves upon water
is the life given
is it love between us

3
In my mind we joined together:

as it rained, as
I was sad in the rain, as
he laid me with his arms

into his shoulder
a joy given into me like sorrow

4
Wulf, Wulf,
        it is not
at all hunger shaking my limbs
but that you do not journey

        absent & yet
        you fill me

5
They take it from me:
        in the manner
of a gift

the spine of a feather, a cloud in the body

        ai, it is
        easily broken, what

was never at one:

you & I, *Wulf,* the one
with the other

& singing

Loss of the Forest

Love is a fact
and black and blue is the skin
of water and sometimes milky white
and the fable always involves a boy with wings
who doesn't care for his biographer
and when the boy comes down to earth
the dogs all run to bite his body.
Here's what to do.
Get in the car and hurtle past the chooks.
Here's what to do. Head for the beach
and sit on the sand till all the people
leave the beach then make
as if to leave yourself. Ah well
at least climb well above the waves
and listen to the little darkness notes
which only sleeping birds outdistance.
Write a song about the wind
and send it to the one you love. The wind
is more important than the forest tra la
though the loss of the forest
would be terrible. Paste some clouds
above the map
and let the wind just puff them out to sea.
Let the ocean liner sail away!
Let them smash the plaster
off your leg with hammers!
And if the boy still yearns to float
then hobble home at once
and tie him to the flagpole
high above the water.

Wellington

It's a large town
full of distant figures on the street
with occasional participation.
Someone buys some shares,
another gets a piece of the action.
Foreign languages are spoken.
A good secretary
is worth her weight in gold.
The man himself
is sitting on a little goldmine.
And down on Lambton Quay
the lads in cars go past, it's raining,
and the boys from Muldoon Real Estate
are breaking someone's arm.
They don't mean harm, really, it's
nobody's business, mainly free
instructive entertainment,
especially if you don't get close
but keep well back like
all the distant figures in the crowd.
So you watch what you can
but pretend to inspect with interest instead
the photographs of desirable private
properties, wondering how close they go
to government valuation. That one's nice.
The question is, do you put your hands
above your head or keep them
in your pockets. Do you want a place
without a garage, could you manage
all those steps. The answer is
the man would simply like you off the streets.
You haven't even got a window
and his is full of houses.

Party Going

It's lonely in the world
when all you get is pity.
The grass is tall and straight
and sometimes waving in the wind.
It grows around the sleeping lovers
and though the police are coming
they somehow look remoter. The last time
I saw you, you said you really
wanted to go home but you had this feeling
you were being followed. You were
half in darkness, half in light,
going outside with all the others.

The Voyeur: An Imitation

How long a minute seems out in the falling snow
and how pale the late Victorian girl is, sleeping
in her bed. How small she is, the same shade
as the curtains, sahib, sleeping even as she chooses.
We look at her but don't 'relate', living too late
in another century. The lighting is soft and clear
but not intense, like a royal court or the modest glow
of a radio at night and really, she is
somehow medieval, quite flat upon the paper.
And we should put the book down now and just return it
to the shelf and then that way at least
be done with it. But that would be too much like
putting down the ancient family pet, not possible,
even if the mind is gone, the form of what was loved
remains, a passive thing demanding to be cherished.
Also, we have not finished reading. We learned our early
slow advances out of books, getting the answers
off by heart before we knew the questions.
The books showed how the bodies grew
though the books themselves weren't bodies.
We put down other questions and passed them
to the front, and that was reproduction.
The trees we saw were diagrams of trees
with bodies underneath. How far away
those bodies seemed, how cold
they must be now beneath the skies, making
their way through snow by word of mouth
and multiplying as they move towards us. It is
probably their life of whiteness we desire
and probably desire is why you stand
behind the curtains, sahib, and I am here
beside you, persuaded I am also in the picture.
How easily we might partake of what is pallid!
Now you are awake and I am not awake

or I am awake and you are not, and anyway the picture
is a theory: the room itself is luminous.
And we can put this pleasant evening down
entirely to experience, whether or not we find
the girl agreeable, whether we choose to make
advances now or climb back through the window,
postponing the moment once again,
whatever it is we go on imitating.

The Caravan

Music is this task you undertake.
It is not painful, more like eating crayons
while you lie in bed with the children,
and probably dark in the end
but at least together. Meanwhile
the body waits, delighted to be waiting:
it also cares for the future.

Do you still remember the future?
How it made a lot of noise for instance?
There was a caravan, everyone was travelling.
There were conversations, now ancient history,
in which we hurled the family
from hand to hand and all set out:
or I believe we meant to.

I believe also there were
photographs and flowers, and that when the music
stopped, the children went on singing. Now
the words are largely lost in song, and song is lost
inside the children. We sometimes hear the voices still,
a catch of absence when we sit at table,
crossing that sea on which the facts alone set sail.

Declining the Naked Horse

The naked horse came into the room.
The naked horse comes into the room.
The naked horse has come into the room.
The naked horse will be coming into the room.
The naked horse is coming into the room.
The naked horse does come into the room.
The naked horse had come into the room.
The naked horse would of come into the room
again if we hadn't of stopped it.

Red Horse

The red crayon makes us
happiest, selected out with care
and making the outline of a horse
when once it's there complete
a rare delightful business;
then colouring the horse in
red as well, occasionally
going over the edge
but mostly filling up the space
without dismay or panic
and reaching in the box
eyes closed for something more or less
surprising for the sky and finding
deepest blue by accident.

Night Windows Carey's Bay

You write a long poem
about how you are sorting yourself out at last
and how at last you say
there'll never be another word
about departure. Look
around you how the moon
tattooes the spaces all around you,
it isn't even dark. In the house
of doors, the doors are open.
In the house of glass, the glass lets in the light.

Children

The likelihood is
the children will die
without you to help them do it.
It will be spring,
the light on the water,
or not.

And though at present
they live together
they will not die together.
They will die one by one
and not think to call you:
they will be old

and you will be gone.
It will be spring,
or not. They may be crossing
the road,
not looking left,
not looking right,

or may simply be afloat at evening
like clouds unable
to make repairs. That
one talks too much, that one
hardly at all: and they both enjoy
the light on the water

much as we enjoy
the sense
of indefinite postponement. Yes
it's a tall story but don't you think
full of promise, and he's just a kid
but watch him grow.

Last Things

The kids want to grow up
and be on the phone and everything.
When they throw stones into the creek
they want to make a decent splash,
they want to get that stranglehold
on water. As usual words of praise
conclude the story we were just
beginning to read
but flipped to the end instead:
the family dog was strong and safe
and underneath himself, no one
was lonely. The stone like stone
hit bottom and was obsolete.

An Outline

First we disowned parents
because they always said *after*;
and friends promised to be around
but were not. Our teachers gave
encouragement and then prescribed
the lonely flower inside the brain.
One showed a picture
but soon would kick the bucket.

At home, away from home, but mostly
nowhere special, we took our own advice.
We got in the car and then just drove
along the road past cliffs and river,
and when we stopped
we slept on the parchment floor,
taking it for the real thing.
We wrote out the poem and slept on it.

Still, there was nothing good for us in words,
or nothing couched in formal English,
while being good itself was good for nothing,
and then again there was always something
coming next, though no particular direction.
The baby lay in its cot and cooed
or it lay afloat in water inside mother.
When once that baby grows, we said,

and put away the car. We built the house then
by the side of the road
at the end of the road beside the river.
Friends came and were welcome
though many failed to make sense
except in pieces, and others
had only rested quietly by mistake.
All day they took their boats

upon the water. We felt alone,
perhaps, but full of promise.
We still possessed the poem in outline,
we had kept some image of the flower in mind.
Now, too, there were provisions, jars of preserves
against the future, photographs to remind
that nothing entered the picture
save cats and children; and the telephone rang

to tell of father's death or just
in other words to ask who's speaking.
We sat by the road and watched
the water tremble as it still stayed perfect.
We woke and slept and that is how
we kept in touch. The children woke in the night
and cried and we sang words to cure.
One crashed the car

and the others soon shot through.
We were young too: we thought
that every goodbye was the last goodbye
and that every last word was made to be careful.
We waved and we waved of course, and now
we find we don't stop waving: believing we see
our life at last, and thinking it over,
knowing how far the road goes home.

A Scottish Bride

Long division and underprivilege,
sweets in a paper twist; or later,
hiking in the hills, days

like the fizz of flowers in a vase
she carried to a neighbour's house,
a war bride with a photograph of home,

and her own house on a single pulse
of stone, lapped by the tidal starlight.
Whose days were those?

A lit hearth, the flames trod water,
and on the dresser a wedding-cake
ascended like a genealogy towards

the two small figures on the top,
standing beside a silver flower
which gave them back a blurred reflection.

Were those the circumstances
which would have to change? A daughter
rehearsed expressions in the mirror,

choosing the face she might prefer to hold,
another touched the perforations
of a stamp, a profile she was saving.

*You cannot imagine, halfway
across the world*, her father wrote,
the sorrow of the undersigned. Was that her mother

then, who made those numbers on a slate?
Were those her children, almost finished eating,
blowing upon their faces in the spoons?

Water, a Stopping Place

There are places named for
other places, ones where
a word survives whatever happened

which it once referred to. And there are
names for the places water comes and touches,
but nothing for the whole. A world

released from reference
is travelling away. Its monotones of swell
surround the modest island nation

where a man and woman
lie together by a stream
on a blanket anchored to the grass

by stones. She has turned a radio on
and as their passion comes to rest
she hears the first commercial break

which advertises cereals, then tractors.
Later she walks down
to fill a bottle from the stream

and stands, bare feet on gravel,
meaning to scoop water out of water,
her dress tucked up. It is late

to be changing the topic of a conversation
but she is searching for a word,
something to tell him why he something huge

about devotion, some other sound beyond
this small dark gargle from the past,
not vowel, not consonant, not either.

Legacies

It was nothing like a legacy.
We didn't know the word.
We dug a hole and buried things in bottles,

a home-made picture dictionary
and seven orange stamps,
an outline map of land and water,

descriptions of our house and school
and things we did there,
news of those days in which we lived.

We laid them deep because they had to last.
Beings with wings would come
in time to come and dig; curious to learn

how people were in that century before
the terrible years of intergalactic war.
Those bottles won't have floated far

but whatever's there by then
will hardly matter. Something
will have made its way through cork

and hatched, and hatched again.
Grubs which grow wings
or eat dark leaf and wood,

stuff rising to the surface leaving
other stuff behind. Things
that eat things! the sizzling colonies,

the meals of afterbirth and rot.
They've got my drawing of a bicycle,
three syllables above two wheels.

She Says

She lived there once where you were once,
in coastal light and gusts of stone.
Eventually, she says, you're left alone,
and the place is a gap in conversation.

She says you find things out in words:
the sadness of the emigrating master
is ornament-in-darkness, another sort

of language. The heart might be
a field or river stranded in a window,
someone carving a boat there. Beautiful

people, the landscapes of a friendly land.
The poor are as passionate as charity,
surviving in everything they spend.

The Distance Between Bodies

Sheets on the floor, a stick
of lipstick on the table,
bits of coastline almost visible at the window.

The distance between bodies
is like the distance between two photographs.
The star on the boy's chest.
The girl's head resting on the star.

Girl Reading

She overhears the sound of things in hiding.
She bites an apple and imagines orchard starlight.
Each time she licks her thumb, its tip,
she tastes the icy branches,
she hears a sigh migrate from page to page.

Zoetropes

A starting. Words which begin
with Z alarm the heart:
the eye cuts down at once

then drifts across the page
to other disappointments.

*

Zenana: the women's apartments
in Indian or Persian houses.
Zero is nought, nothing,

nil – the quiet starting point
of any scale of measurement.

*

The land itself is only
smoke at anchor, drifting above
Antarctica's white flower,

tied by a thin red line
(5000 miles) to Valparaiso.

London 29.4.81

Out West

I was riding one of the best-loved horses in the world.
Hither and yon we went, here and there,
in and out of the known universe.

'There goes Wild Bill,' people said.
'Look at that varmint go!'
There I went.

I went straight to the dictionary
and looked up varmint.
'What's it say?' said a friend. 'What's it say?'

I thumbed through the pages.
'Vermin,' I said, 'vermin
with an excrescent t.'

'Well doggone,' said someone,
and it's true, the dog was gone,
lost in the gulches and the sages,

leaving just me and the horse,
a couple of ornery critters
who might just as well mosey along,

crossing the ford by starlight,
and miles away, the woman –
lonely and beautiful – waking to find us gone.

Magasin

I have brought my father
things to read, *Pix*, *Post*, *People*,
and I tell him how *magazine*

is like the word for shop
in French. I have just started high school,
I am learning a language.

My father lifts his striped
pyjama top so I can see
what looks like the map of Africa

where the doctor has traced
the shape of his liver
for the third-year students.

At the end of the ward
men are listening to the races
and from the next-door bed

the man with one leg,
the bloke my father says
might have to lose the other,

leans across to tell my father
something about
the second leg at Trentham.

Jalopy: the end of love

Do you drive an old car?
Or a jalopy?
Now where could that word come from?

Somewhere in the world
someone you know
must be driving a jalopy.

As for you, one day you are out
on a country road
miles from the sort of place

that might be miles from anywhere
and your car breaks down.
Well, it's an old car.

And somewhere in the world
someone you used to love
has that ancient photograph of you

sitting behind the wheel
high on the Coromandel.
It's a jalopy.

Just at the moment though
it doesn't want to start.
Whatever it is, it's finished.

Our Father

for Charles Causley

On one trip he brought home
a piece of stone from the river,
shaped like a child's foot

and filled with the weight
of the missing body. Another time
he just walked in

with our lost brother
high on his shoulders
after a two-day absence;

and it seems like only yesterday
he was showing us
the long pole, the one

out there in the yard now,
taller than twice himself,
that still hoists

our mother's washing out of reach.

Milky Way Bar

I live at the edge of the universe,
like everybody else. Sometimes I think
congratulations are in order:
I look out at the stars
and my eye merely blinks a little,
my voice settles for a sigh.

But my whole pleasure is the inconspicuous:
I love the unimportant thing.
I go down to the Twilight Arcade
and watch the Martian invaders,
already appalled by our language,
pointing at what they want.

Masturbating

Poor boy. Here he is,
home from Bible Class.

He closes the door.
He lifts the mattress
and takes out the book with dog-eared pages.

Whenever I think of him,
I half remember Gaynor
who used to go out
with the local stock-and-station agent.

She was a teacher
but she couldn't spell –
a girl from Christchurch
doing her country service.

She said the trouble was
she took after her father
and he was a bit touched.

For example, she could remember
when she was a child.

'Here is the church,' he would say,
'and here is the steeple;
open the door
and there are the fingers.'

My Lost Youth

'My lost youth
as in a dream,'
begins this poem

beginning with a line
in what I think is Polish

★

glimpsed

on a sheet of paper
in the ticket-office
at the bottom of the cable car.

Two men behind glass
are bending over it,
the careful, mysterious

copperplate of Polish,
the English lightly
pencilled in above . . .

Of course there is more to it
than my lost youth,

★

patches of pain and love,
a page from start to finish,

but you can hardly go on looking,
and tourists are lining up

★

and someone punches
your new downtowner

and through you go
and leave the poem behind –

keeping in mind a phrase or two
as you travel backwards up the hill

★

to alight at last

above the wooden town
they've nearly finished tearing down
to make the city . . .

★

something about desire perhaps,
something about desire,
the fears . . . or fires . . . of youth,

★

'her mortal gown of beauty' . . .

Miscarriage

In the year most of the girls
started wearing bright colours,
my youngest daughter wore gray.
She sat up late, reading the paper,
nursing her terrible temper.

A lot of it slips
my mind now, but one night
her beauty slowly dawned on me;
then dawn came too
and her place was empty.

Where had she gone?
Was she lost in the headlines?
I think she must have slipped out
while I was reading something
over her shoulder.

Breaking the Habit

Even the children lend a hand,
stealing from room to room,
wrapping your smoke-rings in a towel.

Hirohito

I am like a canary whose cage has been
opened and someone says: 'Fly away!'
Where should I fly to? If I have a song
to sing, why should I waste it on places
where the wind may blow it away?

To improve his eyesight
the young Hirohito gazes
at the horizon every day.

Birds and clouds: one day
he will be a living god.

★

In the playground
he always has to be leader;
the other kids
line up behind.

Already he knows
about physical fitness,
the importance of the will.

He likes insects, plants and butterflies.
He admires
the delicate protocols of Nature.

★

One day his father went mad:
he peered at his people
through the paper telescope
of his own speech.

Hirohito watched his father
being taken away
and thought of jellyfish.

*

At the age of 20
he travelled to Europe.

In London he sat for Augustus John.
He played golf
with the Prince of Wales.

In Paris his knowledge
of European military history
amazed the generals of France.

The happiest days of his life.

Hirohito went home to Japan,
ate eggs and bacon,
and dressed like a Western gentleman.

*

Then there was the war:
about which we know the truth
or do not know the truth,

in which Hirohito either played
the leading part
or he did not.

Perhaps he was
just a puppet of his warlords.

Or perhaps they lined up behind him
while he stared at the horizon

and the sun rose
and the sky filled with planes.

★

Hirohito knew everything
and nothing. 'Let the cry
be vengeance!' cried the allies.
'If you meet this man, don't hesitate.'

Hirohito hid inside the palace air-raid shelter,
a bank vault
with ten-metre thick
ferro-concrete walls.

★

When he announced the surrender
his ministers wept:
the god's voice
being broadcast on the radio.

At first no one could understand Hirohito.
He spoke a language of his own.

And for two days the nation wept –
long enough to let the Emperor's chamberlain
replace the bust of Napoleon
in his study

with one of Lincoln.

★

They say that when he met MacArthur
Hirohito bowed so low
that the handshake took place
high above his head.

So the Son of Heaven was a family man after all –
not in the least divine,
just a quiet marine biologist
able to sign the instruments of surrender.

★

I am writing my book about him,
A Modest History of the Wind,
but I am in difficulty:

chapter after chapter
is being blown away.

There he is: the warrior on a white horse –
blown away.

And there: the Shinto priest
planting rice seedlings
in the palace gardens.

Gone.

And look: there is Hirohito
winding his Mickey Mouse watch.
Tick-tock: the wind takes him.

Petals blown away –
as in a haiku,
as in a tanka.

★

In this final chapter, a funeral:
the powers of the world
have gathered in mourning.

Hirohito –
the 124th occupant
of the Chrysanthemum Throne.

Glancing idly at the news
I catch sight of him through snow,

a man with glasses
staring out of the screen
of my 14-inch Sanyo.

Brazil

1

All night Brazil approached you through the dark.
The light behind mountains
was the light in the silver-merchant's eyes
two villages down river, was the blade
his father's father gave him, years ago,
to help him strike a deal with strangers.
His great right arm struck you
once, struck you twice,
because you had no money.
He watched you walk towards Brazil.

Brazil was women buying food from men,
the directions water followed.
Brazil was stars above the water-raft,
the parchment and the livestock where you slept,
and in the morning you woke and travelled on,
Brazil was where you were going.

Years later, a thousand miles away,
the place was still Brazil,
was still a single-minded journey,
the turmoil of a single coin ungiven,
the silver there in your hand.

2

The people of the second river
announced themselves by clapping;
you entered every village to applause.
You filmed their dances, the bodies
moving to the sound of waterfalls
a little way downstream. You watched
their life go on by word of mouth.
The dance of men with cattle,

of manioc and chicken, the dance of Elvis,
the dance of cattletrucks and pastry.

★

The boy turned to the Senator.
One thousand feet below the copter
you could see the white flashing of water
mixed with the bright grins of bandits.
'Bad country,' he said. 'Poisonous spiders.'

3
Papers on a desk, a river,
and around each bend in the river
Brazil replaced Brazil.
It was a funny idea, she thought:
tampons in the jungle.

Papers on a desk safeguarded the desk.
You sat in a chair while the man there
told you his problems: no village,
no machinery, no available women.

★

The captain sat in his chair while the man
told him his problems. Outside
engines shunted in the yard.
Brazil was several photographs of feathers.
Brazil was urgent measures, which ended
when we disappeared from sight. And around
each bend in the river, Brazil replaced Brazil.
You looked at your ticket: the picture
of birds, the single word, *Brazil*.

4
Take-offs and delays.

Brazil was a rough airstrip in the jungle.
Near the runway, parrots chattered on a log.
He watched the woman spray her hammock
with insecticide, and sat beside her as she slept.
She tossed and turned in the black waters
and white waters of her sleep, imagining
an angel made of bricks. The colonel
came down the path towards them,
already screwing the top off the bottle.
This was more like it! Manioc and chicken
and, if they were lucky, ice-cold lager.

The suitcase was filled with batteries.
Mr Sunday sang on the radio,
a girl waved her Davy Crockett hat.
The explorers sprayed their hammocks
hoping to get a good night's sleep.
Short powerful men demanded cigarettes.
Nose flutes, necklaces of teeth.
She kept glancing at their genitals.
What would she do with so many nose flutes?

She sprayed her hammock with insecticide.
This time, surely, a good night's sleep.
'I'll just knock on the door,' he said.
The senator himself answered, delighted to see them.
Before they were seated, he had taken
the top off the brandy.

5
The secret tribe knew a secret tribe
but would not say. 'Do you mean deeper
in the jungle?' he demanded, beginning to get angry.

But they would not say. The woman
swam, anyway, not caring about the crocodiles.

Butterflies settled on the old Vauxhall Velox.
The word for the snakes was viridescent.
She worried about their driver's bandaged hands.

6
God floated above the Amazon.
He dreamed of Europe under sail.
He thought of the pre-Columbian sky,
and Portugal with cities in its stomach.
He placed a conference of spiders on the track.

★

Brazil, he wrote, was tribe after tribe
attached to stone, windows which rose
above the poverty of beef, everyone eating.

And everything you admired, the people
gave you. This child, this river,
all these trees.

7
'So many birds and I yearn to see seagulls.'
She wrote such things in her diary.

Brazil was the way
her memories all deserted her
and then came back, frightened,
full of apology, asking to stay.

★

Oh her eyes are black, far down,
like stones below a bridge.
Her hair is long, or short,
the way hair is . . .

★

'Can you imagine
this place?' said the young American,
who already thought he would stay.

He turned off the radio.
'It's like there are 500 words for jungle
and only one for flame.'

The man at the FUNAI post nodded.
He went on reading Shakespeare.

8
Brazil would watch the jungle murder sleep
and then perhaps sing on.
Brazil was happy, Brazil
was the great intolerable lines of song
a peasant offered on a piece of stone.

★

Look! They watched
the canoe sing on through the foaming waters.
God was on fire above the Amazon.

★

'There is a place,' sang Mr Sunday,
'beyond the barricades of stars . . .'

★

He turned off the radio
and gave the boy the two batteries.
Muito obrigado. He spoke some Portuguese,

but probably he would never understand
the music he held there, just for a moment,
in the palm of his hand.

9
We filled the suitcase with cigarettes.
The Indians ran towards us.
The Amazon flamed and we shielded our eyes.
The water foamed, it wandered
like the edges of lace, it travelled across
the high wide cheekbones of our race.

*

'Help, look at the time,' said the missionary.
He turned on his heel and was gone.
So this was Brazil.
He stepped out of Brazil, or into Brazil.
He stepped out of the half-built cathedral
and simply vanished into the jungle.

Phar Lap

Unlikely combinations,

Prayer Wheel and Winkie, Sentiment
and Radium: names that contract and expand
like a big heart pumping

till you get an unlikely starter,
this chestnut colt,
foaled in Timaru, October 4 1926,

by Night Raid out of Entreaty,
with Carbine somewhere
in the background.

*

The hide is in Melbourne,
the heart in Canberra.
The bones are in Wellington,

the big delicate skeleton
of a horse
who used to mean business.

*

Can the name
have been planned as a pun?

In English it is one thing.
In Siamese, Lightning.

And they say it means
something in Egyptian.

★

But he was virtually unbeatable,
the big fellow,
winning race after race in Australia
and never fading,

even after they shot at him,
even after they missed,

★

even after he died in America
of intestinal tympany,
of theory after theory . . .

They say that for five days he ate
pasture sprayed with lead arsenate,

they say that his Australian strapper
gave him Fowler's Solution,
incorrectly mixed,

or maybe even the Mafia . . .

Well, let's say he died in California,
let's say he died of absence

★

and that when they stopped talking
they sent him home,
made him articulate
bone by bone

★

till one day up at the Museum,
it might be fifty years later,

wandering along
past the days of pioneer settlement,

I walk past Cook's cannon
and a case of muskets

and hear a woman sing
in another language

from the far side of Phar Lap's ribcage.

Remarkables
for Janet Frame

Mountains in boxes,
years of people.

And then she smiles.
'Let me look.' Look up

and over and under
while the blue apple-paper,

the peaks and snow, those
eyes that still gaze and water

once again
get themselves ready.

from Isabella Notes
for Harry Orsman

Isabel, three syllables,
or four, *Isabella*, a village
between two castles, each

high on its hill, and the light
still there in the evening
when she rides out on her favourite horse,

the one that is pale, its mane
like the snuff-coloured moth
whose wings shiver

at the dark sound of *guitar*.
One day Granada will fall,
one day it will be all

Isabel and Ferdinand
and God: Castile this side
of the ruined wall, on the other

Alhambra, and the artist painting
the girl's face, a mist
in front of the eye, children at school,

all things bright, and beautiful.

My Sunshine

He sings you are my sunshine
and the skies are gray, she tries
to make him happy, things
just turn out that way.

She'll never know
how much he loves her
and yet he loves her so much
he might lay down his old guitar
and walk her home, musician
singing with the voice alone.

Oh love is sweet and love is all, it's
evening and the purple shadows fall
about the baby and the toddler
on the bed. It's true he loves her
but he should have told her,
he should have, should have said.

Foolish evening, boy with a foolish head.
He sighs like a flower above his instrument
and his sticky fingers stick. He fumbles
a simple chord progression,
then stares at the neck.
He never seems to learn his lesson.

Here comes the rain. Oh if she were only
sweet sixteen and running from the room again,
and if he were a blackbird
he would whistle and sing
and he'd something
something something something.

Colloquial Europe

Mr Sharp gets out of the taxi.
He doesn't smoke but lights his pipe.
His various friends walk up and down.
'And this? What do you call this?' says the driver.
'In the land I come from,' says Mr Sharp,
'it is called a taxi.' Then he waits on the quiet platform.

'Good seats but a bad train. Don't you think?'
Someone is speaking. 'And that trunk beside you,
is it heavy?' 'Heavy? Why, yes,
it is heavy, inside it I have the whole
city of Budapest.' 'Ah Budapest! always
so beautiful; myself I am travelling west.'

And it's so strange to stroll from the train
straight into the capital. There are not many houses
in the little street, just a boy eating a crayon.
He has visited his uncle, a village far in the hills,
traversing the woods beyond the stormy river.
Now he is home. He opens the door and explains.

You see a courtyard beyond the courtyard
and remember the work of a well-known artist:
a scatter of clouds in the sky, and sunlight
on the fine new library – 'one that will surely hold
all of our books.' And beyond there are pinewoods,
included, of course, to make the picture perfect.

'A few leaves, a few clouds, and
the fat doctor was halfway up the stairs.'
How my heart sank when I saw him!
But he behaved magnificently, unlike
I must say, my publisher, who is pleasant enough
but won't even glance at my poetry.

Now here is my coffee, just as I like it.
The town is still whole, and very interesting,
and my leg is well again, thank you,
after my recent trip to Australia. The mist
will be gone by the weekend. We shall sing
and stroll in the surroundings

for Autumn is always pretty in these parts,
black smoke on the trunks,
old towns with towers and medieval houses,
and then there is always the Spring:
I like to wait for my late lady friend
whenever the ice on the Danube is breaking.

He carries the lady's fur on his arm.
He has already waited for seventeen minutes,
eyeing the five or six plain girls who are also waiting.
So sad that this is only a Hungarian lesson.
But my dear fellow, it goes without saying.
It goes without saying.

Well, he sent her a postcard but, the fool,
he should have known she wanted a letter!
On what trivialities it depends, whether one takes a wife.
I suppose I should write all this down.
Now let us stroll with our valuables,
as no one here is inclined to be punctual.

'He was always speaking of the Great Powers,
my thoughtful young friend; so much of a hurry.
Why he almost . . .' But look, the porter
holds out his empty hand. 'What,
please, is this?' 'Ah, in New Zealand,'
says Mr Sharp, 'we call that the tip. Taxi!'

Hence the pale, hopeless voice of the waiter,
who knows that my soup tastes like a ticket
for a magnificent cruise on the Danube.
Ah my love, on the coast of the past
and desiring to make your acquaintance,
tell me, where shall we dine tonight?

But now I prefer my Hungarian lesson,
so we want none at all of this music.
'The hotel is nice with rather small rooms
and we left a few coins on the table;
then the waiter came and took the cutlery, yes,
while the bread it remained in the basket.'

And see, our friends, smiling and chatting,
have already left the garden. They argue
whether the Chain Bridge is older,
and therefore a little more beautiful. Why?
Curd tart or poppy noodles? Of course you do.
Goodbye, goodbye, goodbye . . .

'A tranquil place, but I really preferred it
in Linz.' Her impertinent nose
which I glimpsed through the powder.
And now this wonderful night at the theatre.
We sit in the clumsy audience,
and kiss a great deal as the great curtain rises.

Ain Folks

On the road between Aye and Och Aye
the days I was searching
for word of my ancestors

I heard a bit of a song beginning
over by the side of the road. It was
my grandfather somewhere

beyond the railway line
calling and waving, coming to say
he won't buy me a bicycle.

No, he says, no; and then writes
it in a letter – after which I suppose
there's something about the weather.

★

Well I never knew him anyway,
first boy with a bike in all Derry
says my mother, who also tells

how he ran off with the blacksmith's daughter,
a girl who went to her own wedding
but never to one of her children's

★

certainly not to my mother's,
who took her Chemistry degree
to a hotel bar about an inch

above Antarctica, while he kept on riding
to his signal box out on the line
between Edinburgh and Kings Cross,

keeping his eye on the time,
the pure slog of rails up the incline,
the two making their way together

★

till they pause at the level crossing there
and he quietly switches the points
from yon bonnie banks

to the likewise purple heather.

The English Teacher

My mother was teaching Polish soldiers.
Each day at four o'clock they marched down to the school.
This was in Scotland, Prestonpans, near Edinburgh.
'Salt pans,' says my mother, 'the monks
would make salt in the pans.'

They needed the language for the invasion of Europe;
also they wanted to meet people.
Everyone likes to get along socially.

There was a dashing sergeant.
He had only the one word of English.
At the end of each class, he clicked his heels,
opened a silver case and said, 'Cigarette?'

But my mother didn't smoke.
She stood at the blackboard, cleaning off phrases.

'Just words,' she says, 'only expressions.'
I am a soldier. I am your friend.
My mother was in her late twenties.
'I didn't know your Dad then.'

He was in San Francisco
in a nightclub called 'The Lion's Den',
or he was waking at dawn in the State of Nevada
on a train crossing America . . .

while among the Poles there was one,
a sad man who stood out from the bunch;
the Russians had locked him away,
back when they were still helping Hitler.

He had been a carpenter.
But his wife and children,
they might be dead, might be anywhere,
he might never know where they were.

The long trains laboured south
with their troops and ammunition:
two engines in front, and one at the back.

The soldier made a wooden plaque
and left it with my mother;
also a thank you letter . . .

'Give me more detail,' I say.
'You know, to put in the poem.'

But what happened to the plaque,
my mother can't remember.
'It was lovely,' she says.
All she recalls is the carpenter's sadness.

The letter she carried all the way to New Zealand,
till somewhere in the South Island,
shifting from place to place,
packing or unpacking, somehow she lost it.

Someone had written it out for him,
maybe one of the officers.
Yours faithfully, it said, or yours sincerely,
and every last word was set down correctly.

Moonlight
Kate Gray (1975–1991)

I start up a conversation
with occasional Kate. Too late,
too late, but with a big sigh
she appears in the sky.

I tell her the home doesn't forget –
her mother's lullaby step
still reaches the chair
where her father sits deep in the forest.

I hear myself saying
please and please and please;
I want to go back
to the start of the nineties.

Sleepless night, big almond eyes,
and a hand rocks a pram in the passage;
from somewhere a long way
outside of our houses

the moon sends its light to this page.

Picnic at Woodhaugh
Dunedin: 1863

In the half light of the Early Settlers Museum
there is a world of trees; they rise
on their roots to steal the sun.

But there is no sun.

A small bridge negotiates the stream:
a log and rail, with steps at either end,
a stile across a fence of water.

★

Men and women
in a Dunedin clearing
detailed off

behind a long white cloth
where four plates and half-a-dozen bottles
represent the feast.

Dark nineteenth-century light
but enough still there to show us
where the light has been . . .

Each figure has a face, a small one,
and they all face out. They
seem to have finished eating.

★

Fifty good folk at a picnic –
the men mostly standing, the ladies afloat
on the grass with their children –

plus two who have come to the front:
a woman dressed as a man, black trousers,
and, perched on her lap, a fellow in tails.

They are performers, perhaps?
Or even the most important guests?

They stare straight out like all the rest.

★

The exhibition catalogue says
that 'looming verdure threatens
to engulf the group'.

And it is true: they are tiny
and trite among the trees:
safely ashore, yet still at sea.

★

They know how to stand
on the deck of a ship approaching land . . .

★

There are strollers elsewhere in the park,
some lost in a world of shade,
fading or about to fade

★

two of whom manage to be clear –
latecomers, they cross the bridge
and aim for the middle of the canvas,

pausing only to admire the first recorded
Dunedin dog: a trunk on legs, eyes on a snout,
elephant ears, tail sticking out

★

though in fact the dog is walking with them

★

and the man looks faintly embarrassed,
as if stepping across
the surface of a trampoline.

★

His knees are too near the ground,
and he compensates with a puzzled forward lean:
the incline, perhaps, of thoughtful conversation,

or of someone planning to found a nation

★

while she . . .

★

but really, she can hardly hear . . .
What was that he said?

★

And it is so *very* hard to see –
and so she takes his arm and advances

holding aloft her *parasol*

*

which like her, she thinks, is pretty but unexpected

a fresh flower of the forest,
a wee bit smaller than her head.

What to Call your Child

Veronica's heart belongs to her
and not to Troy. Thus the boy
lives in slow disaster, by smoke
and scattered sand; he stands in the gray water
or stalks the shore,
and when Veronica's heart
is washed up there, he doesn't love her
any more. Thus guitar joins guitar
and she is there at last in the ocean
but now he doesn't want to kiss her;
in fact he hates his sister. Oh she is herb,
she is skin, Christ in his skeleton,
the whole of the world he wants,
maybe jasmine. She knows the quietest name
of the wind, and says it but he cannot hear.
He makes a bird of paper (bird of timber,
bird of trees) and throws it to the breeze.
He places his foot inside his father's shoe
and listens to his mother talking:
'Grace has come back and Olive will be, too.'

A Final Secret

Every morning, we the Loop say:
'Will you enter creation?
I will enter creation.'
Then we have breakfast.

It is better if one Loop asks the question
and the next Loop answers,
and thus around the room,
especially if there are many Loop present,
until you are done. But if you are alone,
you may question yourself
and make your answer in a somewhat different voice.

Or you can use the same one, it is entirely your choice.
We the Loop do not make love any more,
we do not make decisions,
but we travel and explore, loving unlikely distance.
We have been called a nomadic nation.
We are always getting into our stride.

Today we crossed the sea of Dunedin, the great pedestrian
        waters.
We elbowed so many people aside.
We were in haste. We had heard
of another branch of the Loop, perhaps a tribe,
or perhaps it was only a village,

and, as fully expected, we woke on another shore.
The sun was shining on the wet sand, on the sails,
and somewhere ahead lay the heart of the nation.
Will you enter creation?
I will enter creation.

Visiting Mr Shackleton

for Chris Cochran

Cool! Wow! Beautiful! Awesome!
Like going back in time.
Amazing! Historic! Finally
I am truly blessed.

Wow! History! Fantastic!
Wonderfully kept.
Shackleton's the man!
Like going back in time.

Wow! Cool! Historic! Yo!
Awesome! Privileged. Unreal!
And Thank you, God. And Happy
Birthday, Dad. And Thailand.

Antarctic Stone

in my hand
and the spine of a hill
inside the stone

dark ridge of earth & bone
then inclines and heights
and sudden drops

where whatever pours
is wind, is ice, forgetting itself
at last in light

in quiet line, horizon

The Next Thousand

There'll be the same non-stop palaver
about who did or did not invent the pavlova.
Something like China will rise,
some sort of Empire fall –
not that we will much care, not being here at all.
Deep inside the organism there'll be the familiar orgasm.
So certainly something should happen.
Possibly arithmetic and frost
will tiptoe right to the edge of the forest;
the wild blue yonder may simply go west.

The lovetorn boy will descend
from topmast and tempest
and try to get something off his chest.
He'll stare into her eyes. Big skies.
Big skies. As for the puzzled past,
it will just get longer and longer
and generally there'll not be all that much left to squander;
though someone like Hillary
will probably climb something like Everest,
because something will probably be there.

But we won't care. Someone will work his way
up the touchline. Someone will be sighing and sighing.
Someone will soon give up trying.
Someone will make an improper suggestion.
Someone will stumble over the body in question.
Someone will want to be Moslem or Christian.
The one you love will be one in a million,
no one will visit the red pavilion;
but someone will care for the one who wept,
someone will note how the world is windswept.

There will be no more screens or screen-savers
but I believe there will still be pages.
March will give way to the furious winter's rages,
the dark night to the new day,
the schedule to the resumé. I'm sorry to say
things sometimes will and sometimes will not be
exactly what they used to be. Many words
will be thoroughly meaningless:
say goodbye to sound-byte and mini-series,
but not to miseries.

At the end of the day there'll be a pretty big ask
but not a big answer. Pines will march across
paddocks and pasture. Someone will take
someone else to task. And listen to this:
there'll be an amazing invention which might replace
        batteries.
Actually, no one will know what the fact of the matter is,
and hems will be down. Almost certainly.
The bad girl's parents will go to town.
There will be no cars but much traffic congestion.
There will still be press conferences. Next question?

Authors who stay in print will include Dickens and
        Nostradamus.
There'll be maybe a dozen more Dalai Lamas.
There'll be an amazing invention which could well replace
        pyjamas.
Someone will be out of his depth but go hell-for-leather.
Someone will be at the end of her tether.
There will be such astonishing light on the water.
The sheep will still go like lambs to the slaughter.
Some will hold back while others go racing ahead.
No one will remember our old blue shed.
Both of my children will be dead.

So goodbye to the one who knows no regrets,
who will surely be sorry; goodbye to the thundering lorry.
And goodbye to those long millennial lists,
all of the 'this and that' and 'this and this'.
And let us be glad that the big, repetitive world persists,
so safe, so dangerous . . . As for the lovers,
see how she saves him each time he rescues her,
see how they search the sky for news of weather:
such wide horizons, such amazing cloud . . .
the two coasts crushing the interior . . .

Without Form

for Marion

It is noisiest here in this middle place,
cries of despair and those of praise,
yet you might close your eyes and begin to walk forward.

This must be how the first god did it.
It was back at the beginning, and he began to sing,
though the light – which was there – showed nothing.

The God's Journey

After many years it was necessary to travel there again. He made certain preparations. He attended to the birds. He studied the five maps, each suggesting a different road. One was all paths, which tiptoed across highways after dark. One was coastal: it followed an abandoned railway line, then slipped inland. Another went into the forest, and though it showed a particular route, the legend advised against it. That one might be best. He would decide in the morning.

At the first house, he took the two young children. One at a time, he would push them before him. The father and mother wept. The father had lost his own young brother and sister in just this way. He had made a song about it.

You are pushed ahead,
towards mountain and ocean.
My brother, my sister, I shall seek you out.
Have courage! I shall find you.

But the father did not find them; nor did he become a singer. Now he stood outside his small house listening to his wife's tears and the faint cries of sheep while his youngest children stumbled forward in front of the stranger's cart. His eldest son also stood beside him. 'Do not fear,' he said. 'I shall find them, father. I shall seek them out.'

The god's cart was distant now. Its wheels made small puffs of dust which, as the distance grew, came to resemble the wings of birds. And now the son ran indoors to fetch something. Time went by. An hour passed, almost a day, the mother continued weeping, and even at dusk the boy had not come out.

Song: Alzon

Alzon hides behind itself.
It talks in Occitan.
The stars above Alzon.
The water beside Alzon.

There is one song,
then always another song.
The pines of the night.
The words of this poem.

He loves her but . . . the way
lies through that tunnel
and across the difficult bridge
by which one enters Le Vigan.

So many people!
Everything is wrong.

The hidden paths.
The tunnelling paths.
Alzon hides behind itself.
It talks in Occitan.

Across Brooklyn

This is the street where they still make coffins:
the little workshops, side by side.
I pass them with my daughter on our walk to the river.

Are we seeking the bridge itself,
or the famous, much-reported view?

A few planks and nails lie around,
and each of the entrances seems to darken.
Far back, out of sight, someone is whistling.

Yes, I suppose we do walk a little faster.
There is a faint noise of hammering, too.

The Ladder

Too short to reach the roof,
too short to threaten important windows,

the ladder lies on its side
behind the house, out of sight.

The ladder lies in the grass,
a different grain in each of its rungs

(and wings on each rung
so where can you place your feet?).

And, as you can see, it is rotten.
Nevertheless, it longs to be lifted.

Opoutere

in memory of Michael King

This is the place of posts.
A man in a boat is checking his lines.

He is out towards the rock
at the mouth of the river,
clear sky above the ocean,
while behind him the estuary is filling
with its acres of shine.

*

Once there were a thousand logs on the water,
jostling for space across Wharekawa,
waiting their turn to be rafted out
to the ships which waited offshore . . .

*

January nineteen-ninety-something,
Michael himself pouring the drinks
as he showed us the photographs; and then
he and Peter Walls sat on the verandah,

the balcony, the deck, of the double house
with its view down over the water,
swapping tales about masters at Silverstream,
Father X and Father Y, and Spiro Zavos,

history and music talking together,
the vast entertainment of learning . . .

And do you remember . . .

*

So that again I stop on the footbridge
(there are swallows)
just to see that everyone's here

(and we are), watching water slide over mud,
a boy suddenly lifting an arm
to see if the crabs still run to their smudges

and they do

and always at last everything follows,
the walk through pines to the beach,
the soft, suspended, hesitating air

and then the great lines of blue-and-white thunder

★

and the dotterel's small whistle,
always vanishing, always leading away
from the wee scrape of sand

where the eggs lay,
and still keeping back for another day
that desperate broken wing display

★

though we at any rate would be making no trouble,
walking on towards Ohui,
where we met an American backpacker who pointed up

at the high, heavy, shuffle of gulls
and said, 'Hey, take care up ahead,
this is hawk country.'

★

A line on the page follows the skyline,
like the last light wandering
inland from peak to peak

until late at night there are stars
and there we are
lying flat on our backs

up in the bush between harbour and pa
to see if the universe
is still connecting its dots

and it is

★

for all of the news was up there,
satellites bright in the dark
with their chatter of business and love,

and star after shooting star
(the beautiful wipe-out of worlds!)
whole civilisations, the failings and fallings,

in the flickering, steady, and once again flickering
always migrating light . . .

★

He has one kahawai, and two trevally.
Oystercatchers patrol the tideline.

Pedantic.
A tui whirrs from pohutukawa to pine.

Enough to be going on with really.

★

Now the bad news is here.
The good news is nowhere.

Everything consoles, and nothing.

Everything goes under the earth,
the old timber, and the new.

What is memory but all of us listening?

— without being precisely sure
to whom one owes gratitude

what we want in the end is understanding.

★

And now I suppose he cuts the motor.
Let the tide do the work!

★

And now there is only the sound of water . . .

★

Here in the place of posts
I think I can just make him out

a man in a boat
rowing across the last half-mile of twilight

Still Life with Wind in the Trees

So much of the planet is fragile:
 things that flap on the line,
stuff on a plate, a car skidding
 over the paddocks . . .

I mean: abrupt, conditional,
 and, as usual,
brief: so that you once again assume your place.
 Yet what if one day you looked out

through the open window
 and saw mortality
in the grey scribble
 of a boy holding an apple?

Fragility. Brevity. Beauty, even.
 Light in available space.
And what's joy?
 Even a pencil will point to it.

for Joanna Margaret Paul, 1945–2003

An Inspector Calls

We tiptoed into the house.
The neighbourhood was quiet as a mouse.

I felt very on edge. The money
was in the oven, not the fridge.

★

I glanced at the note on the piano.
Uh oh, uh oh, uh oh.

★

There's always a point at which a routine enquiry
turns into something else entirely.

I had to shoulder my way in.
The bathtub was simply full of the victim.

Encouragement

Someone encourages us to move.
But if you sit well back, you're not so evident.
The bereaved always go straight to the front.
Do they not need encouragement?

Dogs

I tried to work up a little poetry – 'the ever-restless spirit of man' – 'the mysterious, awe-inspiring wilderness of ice' – but it was no good; I suppose it was too early in the morning.
—Roald Amundsen, The South Pole

'What do you think? Shall we start?' –
'Yes, of course. Let's be jogging on.'

So many dogs! And once they begin barking,
it's goodbye to the peaceful Polar morning.

Yet there is this: dog can be fed on dog,
the feeble go straight to the chosen.

On the 29th we shot the first one, Bone.
He was only a hindrance.

At our first beacon we had to shoot Lucy.
Sad to put an end to this beautiful creature,

but there was nothing else to be done.
Adam and Lazarus were never seen again.

Sara fell dead on the way
without any prior symptom.

13 dogs each, hence we could sit on the sledges
and flourish our whips with a jaunty air.

Each man was to kill his own dogs
to the number that had been fixed.

I remember how shot followed on shot.
A trusty servant lost his life each time.

We opened the dogs and took out their entrails.
One dog found its grave in another's stomach.

Many just ate till they dropped.
We named this place the 'Butcher's Shop'.

The dogs spent the night in eating;
all night there was crunching and grinding . . .

Rex was turned into cutlets.
Poor, faithful Per broke down utterly:

a little blow from the back of the axe . . .
But we slaughtered Svartflekken.

(He looked good but had a bad character,
hence was consumed with satisfaction.)

The same evening we had to finish
the last of our ladies – Else.

She was placed on the top of a great ice-beacon.
On the way home we would share her out.

(She had quite reasonable flesh
once you scraped away a little mouldiness.)

But in the meantime, the Pole! I remember best
our five weather-beaten, frostbitten fists

clutching the flag, and that the dogs
took not the least interest in the regions

about the earth's axis. How can you care
where a meal came from

when all that you leave is the teeth of your victim?
Then soon enough we were 'turning

for home'. The first one killed on this leg
was Lasse, my own favourite.

We shared him among his companions.
Like Lurven, he made fifteen portions.

Nigger had been destroyed
on the way down from the plateau.

And here again was Don Pedro Christophersen,
partly in shadow, yet gleaming in the sun . . .

And all was so still . . .
But we had to kill Frithjof at this camp;

his lungs, quite shrivelled up,
went straight down another's gullet.

And Thor . . . who could not get to his feet . . .
Yes, of course, it is true, sometimes

I feel quite alone. It is hard almost to speak . . .
My best friends bark in my stomach . . .

But then I think:

Come now, harness the team!
Fetch the right lashings!

And I see once again how the whip
haunts the heads of the dogs

Come over here, Bone!

and how the great unknown
spreads out before us – white, always white,

with always a splendid surface.

Erebus Voices

The Mountain

I am here beside my brother, Terror.
I am the place of human error.

I am beauty and cloud, and I am sorrow;
I am tears which you will weep tomorrow.

I am the sky and the exhausting gale.
I am the place of ice. I am the debris trail.

And I am still a hand, a fingertip, a ring.
I am what there is no forgetting.

I am the one with truly broken heart.
I watched them fall, and freeze, and break apart.

The Dead

We fell.

Yet we were loved and we are lifted.

We froze.

Yet we were loved and we are warm.

We broke apart.

Yet we are here and we are whole.

Hotel Emergencies

The fire alarm sound: is given as a howling sound. Do
   not use the lifts. The optimism sound: is given as the
   sound of a man brushing his teeth. Do not go to bed.
   The respectability sound: is given as a familiar honking
   sound. Do not run, do not sing. The dearly-departed
   sound: is given as a rumble in the bones. Do not enter
   the coffin. The afterlife sound: is given as the music of
   the spheres. It will not reconstruct. The bordello sound:
   is given as a small child screaming. Do not turn on the
   light. The accident sound: is given as an ambulance
   sound. You can hear it coming closer, do not crowd the
   footpaths. The execution sound: is given as the sound of
   prayer. Oh be cautious, do not stand too near

or you will surely hear: the machinegun sound, the weeping
   mother sound, the agony sound, the dying child sound:
   whose voice is already drowned by the approaching
   helicopter sound: which is given as the dead flower
   sound, the warlord sound, the hunting and fleeing and
   clattering sound, the amputation sound, the bloodbath
   sound, the sound of the President quietly addressing
   his dinner; now he places his knife and fork together (a
   polite and tidy sound) before addressing the nation

and making a just and necessary war sound: which is given
   as a freedom sound (do not cherish memory): which is
   given as a security sound: which is given as a prisoner
   sound: which is given again as a war sound: which is
   a torture sound and a watchtower sound and a firing
   sound: which is given as a Timor sound: which is given
   as a decapitation sound (do not think you will not gasp
   tomorrow): which is given as a Darfur sound: which is
   given as a Dachau sound: which is given as a dry river-
   bed sound, as a wind in the poplars sound: which is
   given again as an angry god sound:

which is here as a Muslim sound: which is here as a Christian
sound: which is here as a Jewish sound: which is here as
a merciful god sound: which is here as a praying sound;
which is here as a kneeling sound: which is here as a
scripture sound: which is here as a black-wing sound: as
a dark-cloud sound: as a black-ash sound: which is given
as a howling sound: which is given as a fire alarm sound:

which is given late at night, calling you from your bed (do
not use the lifts): which is given as a burning sound, no,
as a human sound, as a heartbeat sound: which is given
as a sound beyond sound: which is given as the sound
of many weeping: which is given as an entirely familiar
sound, a sound like no other, up there high in the smoke
above the stars

Death of a Poet

i.m. Charles Causley

Between the Tamar and the tarmac,
Beneath a tangled sky,
I saw the Cornish poet
Walking by.

He went where wind and water
Will not be overthrown,
Where light and water meet
Boscastle stone.

It was a day in deep November
When the cold came.
The cold sky squandered
Inside his brain.

Who knocks at Cyprus Well?
Who knocks again, again?
'I think it is the visitor
We must not name.'

Oh men who fish are fishing
And men of tin are gone
Yet men will walk on Bodmin
And hear his song.

The great world makes its changes
And yet remains the same;
And poets' verses will unwind
The tangle in the brain.

Kevin

I don't know where the dead go, Kevin.
The one far place I know
is inside the heavy radio. If I listen late at night,
there's that dark, celestial glow,
heaviness of the cave, the hive.

Music. Someone warms his hands at the fire,
breaking off the arms of chairs,
breaking the brute bodies of beds, burning his comfort
surely to keep alive. Soon he can hardly see,
and so, quietly, he listens: then someone lifts him
and it's some terrible breakfast show.

There are mothers and fathers, Kevin, whom we barely
    know.
They lift us. Eventually we all shall go
into the dark furniture of the radio.

The Cave

We found bones at the back of the cave.
I wanted to walk towards you,
to part your hair where I think the grey starts,
but I am not the man who marches,
I am the man who writes with a twig.

Under the bones, there are always more bones,
and always above them the puzzled heart
so that we hover like hunters above confusing earth,
for the quarry has gone in many directions,
and after a while we both stop digging.

Creatures around us are frightened now.
They watch how we stand and face away.
They see we have thoughts, that we are big.
Creatures around us are frightened.
Always these words come out of our heads.

The Victims of Lightning

*A good poet is someone who manages, in a lifetime of standing out
in thunderstorms, to be struck by lightning five or six times; a dozen
or two dozen times and he is great.*
Randall Jarrell

Often they are naked; clothing is scattered
across a field; or trousers and shirt
appear in some nearby village –
a little tattered, waiting to be folded.
Sometimes with women the chemise is scorched,
yet – strange – the dress and petticoats are spared.
As in war, men are in extremest danger.
'His shoes remain on his feet!' cries the wife,
who then begins to weep; and yes, there are boots
at the end of the man's pale body. Height
is always there at the heart of peril:
a shepherd with staff moving among his sheep,
the tall fisherman lifting his rod, those boys
who huddle beneath a tree . . .
all in their way supply attraction. Even a raised umbrella,
black in the sky, means danger.

And lightning will boast about its work.
It likes to leave an illustration.
On one man's trunk, a grove of pines.
On another a flower, or spider's web.
An ancient pear tree is destroyed
yet shows the branches of itself
on the waggoner's wide chest.
And sometimes it leaves us nothing:

it digs a trench and perforates the bones.
Over there, the farmer stands erect
as if he is posing with his cattle . . .
yet, tiptoe across the field, and touch . . .
well, every creature crumbles!

Some who survive wish to be studied.
I show them to my special room,
ask for a poem, or request a song.
They complain of melancholy and despair,
of ringing in their ears, of cramps. No one
retains the charge, though some believe they do.
Some walk with difficulty, others feel it in the brain.
The blind man regains his vision, yet now is deaf.
An imbecile is rendered sane.
A friend reports how lightning struck a church
and only the minister was spared.
The arrow of the belfry flew across the fields.

Nature is full of mystery: ephemeral realm
with permanent effects. And always accumulation
reminds us what is next: thunder in distance, *choc de retour.*
And silence in schoolroom and cathedral . . .
and body like paste, tongue torn from its roots . . .

so that we move to close the open door.
Outside, the poet lifts his pen, and waits.
The widow raises her umbrella.

Velvet

The earliest deer had a number
and a name. And always when we called he came,
165, unlike those others in the paddock,
unlike the skyline or the failure
in the farmer's thumb, which slipped his mind
at some important moment. It is surely
the plural thing, pure need for company,
that makes us chant at the start of every story –
and in many poems, we say, the short line hides
within the longer. Now when they say velvet,
they mean blades and cuts, they mean this powder.
These days I spend my whole day planting trees.
For only a deer in solitude can be a 165,
can turn and be this other thing entire,
a great head watching from the wall.

Song with a Chorus

The child stands
in the moonlight on the moon
and bounces slowly.
His mother tucks him in.
The light tickles his chin a little.
Dear one, dear one.

Illness is here with its puzzling song.
It muddles your mind
yet tells the truth. For a while
the doctor remembers his own youth
when he, too, was cute.
My lovely one.

The moon lists to port
then to starboard. It is
somehow charming, the way
a mother weeps.
The tears repeat slowly.
My dear, my sweet.

A tear hits the forehead:
a piece of that great sea
we witness and respect.
A doctor would once have said *hectic*
but what now to say?
Dear one, my dear.

Meantime the moon is always travelling.
Stones live on its surface.
You throw them and they take an hour to land.
Give me your hand. Hold me.
It goes around the planet.
Oh my dear one.

1950s

My cricket bat. My football boots.
My fishing rod. My hula hoop.
My cowboy chaps. My scooter.
Draughts. Happy Families. Euchre.
Ludo. Snap. My Davy Crockett hat.
My bicycle. My bow and arrow.
My puncture kit. My cat.
The straight and narrow. Fancy that.

Snakes & Ladders. Alcoholics.
Pick-Up Sticks. My comics.
My periscope. My pirate sword.
The ocean main. The Good Lord.
My fort. My raft. My tunnel.
My flippers. My togs. My snorkel.
My magic wand. My colour-changing silks.
My catapult. My kite. School milk.

My xylophone. My knucklebones.
My boxing gloves. My ukulele.
My bubblegum. My bongo drums.
The Royal Tour. Aunt Daisy.
My flat top. My crew cut.
My pack of cards. My tree hut.
My Hornby train. My autograph book.
My secret code. My sideways look.

The Famous Five. The Secret Seven.
Tarzan of the Apes. My idea of Heaven.
The empty sky. Haere mai.
My View-Master. Sticking plaster.
My Go outside and play. My ANZAC Day.
My tip-up truck. My saying fuck.
My Did you not hear what I said.
My Mr Potato Head. My Go to bed.

135

My Do you wanna bet.
My chemistry set. My I forget.
My clove hitch. My reef knot.
My I forgot.
Korea. Measles. Mumps. Down in the dumps.
My Just William. Counting to a million.
The Invercargill March. My false moustache.
The King and I. Reach for the Sky.

My stamps from Spain and San Marino.
The Winter Show. The Beano.
Cinerama. Orange fizz.
My toy soldiers. Suez.
My pocket knife. Eternal Life.
The Black Prince. My fingerprints.
My plink–a–plunk. You dirty skunk.
My plunk–a–plink. Invisible ink.

Frolic

late at night the lake grows
a little more laconic
like it wants not to want

to say something

★

moonlight (she says)

like flower, like
lick of water

like le lac

★

& then the managed river drops away

Quebec

The café was called Quebec. We used to go there a lot.

The first time, well, we simply liked the name. They had nothing local, but you could ask for anything else.

In winter they served up hot, brutal stews, which we ate like soup, using a spoon, and there were rough slabs of some home-made nutty bread. It was all new to us. In summer, the desserts were airy, filled with berry fruit, or made with lemon.

Before it was Quebec, it was Kerouac's. Before that, I think it was Fettucine, and before that it was a bookshop, Tom's Exchange. The man who ran it wore a grey dustcoat; he wasn't Tom. Tom was never there.

This was years before we met. As I recall, the days were long and awkward. You could take in a few coins and a couple of old paperbacks, and come back out with something you hoped might change your life.

Captain Scott

We brought his body ashore in Oamaru.
I was on one oar, Cherry the other.
The ship stood off.
A telegram was sent, and now we all felt left behind.
I was made to sit beside him while he melted.

Visiting Europe

We rush around and look at famous stuff.
Once in the Louvre, late afternoon with my six-year-old son,
– he has truly had enough – we meet the Mona Lisa.
It's 1981. I lift him above the world's admiring heads.
That lady, I say – we don't know why she's smiling.
What do you think she's thinking about?
Money, he says. *Money.*

Toast

There were too many feathers in the portrait.
My wife wasn't a bird!
I spoke to the artist, and once I had said my bit
he removed the things I found absurd.
Now I could see the electric toaster in her lap.
There was smoke, and she was stroking it.

Pussy

The smoke seemed feline
and so I spoke to him again.
Remove the toaster, I instructed.
Think of something else.
I gestured with the gun.

Her feet were too far from her body.
The hay was tidy, and the sky was black.
I gestured with the gun.
He took it out and asked me for his fee.
Then he left our part of the country.

The Lid Slides Back

Let me open
my pencil-case made of native woods.
It is light and dark in bits and pieces.
The lid slides back.

The seven pencils are there, called *Lakeland*.
I could draw a sunset.
I could draw the stars.
I could draw this quiet tree beside the water.

The Wrong Crowd

They shift and shuffle.
They admire the smoke above the stars.
They love old songs with missing voices.
They smoke in darkened bars.

Hence we surrender on the coastal sand.
We raise above our heads our hands.
We address our captors in a language that is theirs.
We wait in the room where scholars wait upon the stairs.

A man calls now across the great, wise hall
and no one answers. He wants to change the world. Not much.
Time for the captain at last to sing –
to go below, to bellow.

Peter Pan

We always tied our Wendy to the mast.
She ran from the stage, then ran back on.
Applause! Oh, sometimes did we hurt her?
Ah well, my friend, we never liked to ask.

Applause went wandering, there was song,
and walking the plank was pleasant, too.
Each time I fell, I thought of you –
the dangerous deeps, and then, 'ere long,

the sudden splash of intermission.
Yet season by season, Wendy changed.
She was a nanny, then a boy with bumps,
a vision; or maybe I mean the other way about.

I drifted from film to musical to drink.
They told me my role was mostly just to shout.
I could fly and play the flute, I think,
though never both at once. A fellow

can only do one feeling at a time –
you imagine a door, and walk straight through.
And under my costume, I was simple lust.
I married Wendy, then I left her. Well, you must.

They tell me my name was Peter Pan.
I spent my whole life falling from my pram.
But we were the thing, the very thing.
Come here, my darling, while I tell you something.

My Childhood in Ireland

I never climbed the hill
or strolled to the end of the pier
to see what the walkers in rain
might be finding out there.

Nor did the book fall open
where Maeve had secretly signed it.
In fact, it never fell open.
Not that I minded: the world

streamed away
wherever the great ships
were going. Far away
there were ways beyond knowing.

I walked back to the house.
My sister's new child was chained
to her breast. She drifted
inside a dark forest.

My father opined while the dog whined.
The television did its best.
While my father opined
the dog licked itself.

Well, you manage to find
what might make you happy.
I went on the Net. I wandered.
Asian bukkake.

The Sick Son

Because a tree was touching a cloud
I hid under my bed. My brother hid under the covers.
Then my mother came in. She hid inside her head.
My father was out in the great world with his axe.
Would he attack the house this time, or just the tree?
'Come out at once,' he called, 'and come out singly.'
When I was little, he sat me on his knee.
He read to me. He read to me.

The Oral Tradition

The oral tradition tore us apart.
It sang in the heart, it chanted of the sun.
It knew the attributes of gods,
naming their triumphs one by one.
We looked far out: that ship was like a bird!
Its sails were wings beneath the stars.
And kennings like swans would visit from afar
to teach us to be travellers.

Such noise, so many voices!
The oral tradition was absurd.
It knew where killings had occurred.
It said it could cure the damaged sky.
It poured a Scotch, and made the roofbeams sigh.
It always knew which horse to back.
It loved the work of Kerouac.
It said that we would die.

And always it tore us two apart.
It gathered on the terraces and in the stands
– we lingered on the stairwells of the heart –
and true to form the game went on.
Someone was carded, another player scored.
The oral tradition roared and roared
– such noise! so many voices! –
then left to join the fighters at the ford.

Soon it returned with iceplant for a wart.
It passed some comments on my school report.
It sang of the kayak and the waka,
it chanted above the creatures of the water;
it gossiped, and stank of honeydew,
and sniggered whene'er I spoke of you.
It said it knew a man who knew a man who said.
It placed this dark caesura in my head.

At night we heard it make lament.
It summoned the battlefields of France,
and killing fields in Africa and Spain,
the topless and the falling towers,
and armies marching over damp terrain,
and suicidal men who flew from shore to shore,
who could not think in metaphor,
and I believe we wept full sore.

We turned to books and parchment then,
touching a word to turn the page.
The oral tradition grew enraged.
Carving the eagle! A bright blade rose
and now some poor scribe's lungs
lay there beside his bare elbows.
The oral tradition loved such woes.
It called a dozen talkback shows.

Such noise! So many voices!
The oral tradition crept from tree to tree.
It sat small children on its knee.
It held out its glass, and said, When I say when.
And then, and then, and then, and then –
it whispered that you betrayed me with my friend;
then warbled about the afterlife
and said that you would never be my wife . . .

Thus we awoke in the smoky hall at dawn,
and there I assailed you loud and long.
You wept and wailed, and the oral tradition chanted on,
building its blind and paratactic song.
I walked away. The oral tradition
offered up a prayer; I heard it cry: *We're out of here!*
Such noise, so many voices . . . I think I heard
you calling, but I could not hear.

The Ruin

Storm roared in the roof: a rocking of towers.
Giants stood then stumbled.
Once they strode into weather and wind.
Where stairs went down, only these mounds.

Then more is missing.

Walk toward the baths: they are missing.
Toward ramparts and ring-hall: missing.
Toward Romans and Saxons:
missing and missing.

Each man under-taken.
Generation and generation.

Here is a gate made of frost,
Here tiles were torn away and [missing].
Here was fire. Here was [lost]

And here is the true charred text.
See how the ruin rides among riddles
– anchor and inkhorn and loom –
bumping against whatever happens next.

Oh earth went over them all:
chalice and harp, husband and wife,
palace and tented place.

Grey moss on red stone . . .

And here and there a glance, a *gleam*

a home [but missing]

dwelling we almost glimpse across the water.

The Schoolbus

This is the place where the schoolbus turns.
The driver backs and snuffles, backs and goes.
It is always winter on these roads: high bridges
and birds in flight above you all the way.
The heart can hardly stay. The heart implodes.

The heart can hardly stay. The heart implodes.
The body gets down and walks across a field.
There are mushrooms – as in stories,
as in songs. They grow near rabbits.
Slope of hillside,

slant of rain – and here we are again:
a green-roofed house behind the trees.
The body gets down and walks across a field.
The house is full of homework fed by sleep.
A boy combs his hair, brushes his teeth,

or climbs to the top of the valley.
The sky is handkerchiefs, a single shirt.
He wants to climb higher, into a cloud.
He wants to climb into a cloud.
Whatever else is somewhere up ahead.

The schoolbus is driving through the night.
Whatever else is somewhere up ahead.
A boy keeps on hitting his head.
The small girls sing. It's nothing.
We don't know what we mean.

Is that another drink the man is pouring?
The boy turns the handle of the separator.
Cream. The boy stands on the railway line,
disappearing in rust and shine.
Goodnight Irene. Goodnight Irene.

The big door closes. A voice in the kitchen
says: Enough's enough. Running a bath.
Always cold water, boiled in pots.
The driver swears, and then he coughs.
The big door closes and you can't get off.

The Question Poem

Was there a city here?

We were sitting with friends. It was a sunny day.
We were boasting about the local coffee.
Strange self-congratulations, flat whites.
These were friends we had only recently
found our way back to. For a long time
we were far apart.

Did you all survive?

On that first day of school, I mostly remember
being terrified: the dark interior, the children in rows
at their separate desks, and I was now to be one of them.
In a field by the school, there were bales of hay.
I remember inkwells.
That was perhaps a harder day.

Did you hear the bells ringing?

I keep trying to remember.
Somehow I learned to write my way round things.
The teacher made circles on the blackboard
and none of us said a word. Rubble,
then revelation: inside, we were stumbling.
And at the end of the day we all went home.

Did you all survive?

We will never sit in such places again.
A father chasing his small daughter,
both of them laughing.
The girl, a toddler, was calling out, *No, no, Matilda!*
Perhaps she knew the song from somewhere
but I think that must have been her name.

Old Man Puzzled by His New Pyjamas

I am the baby who sleeps in the drawer.
Blue yesterday, and blue before –
and suddenly all these stripes.

Index of Titles

Index of First Lines